Visit us at **www.kidsbooks.com**

Here we are at Santa's World Headquarters at the North Pole.

SEARCH FOR SANTA AT HIS HEADQUARTERS AND...

- ☐ Balls (3)
- ☐ Banana peel
- ☐ Candy canes (4)
- ☐ Dogs (2)
- ☐ Drummer
- ☐ Envelope
- ☐ Gingerbread house
- ☐ Goose
- ☐ Hammock
- ☐ Hearts (2)
- ☐ Igloo
- ☐ Jack-in-the-box
- ☐ Kite
- ☐ Lips
- ☐ Partridge in a pear tree
- ☐ Pick
- ☐ Pillow
- ☐ Rabbit
- ☐ Sandwich
- ☐ Skier
- ☐ Sleeping tree
- ☐ Sleigh
- ☐ Snowballs (3)
- ☐ Snow shovels (2)
- ☐ Snow women (2)
- ☐ Snowmen (2)
- ☐ Stars (4)
- ☐ Stocking
- ☐ Sunglasses
- ☐ Tepee
- ☐ Tricycle
- ☐ Wreaths (2)

Santa's elves work very hard to make sure the toys are ready by Christmas Eve.

SEARCH FOR SANTA IN THE ELVES' WORKSHOP AND...

- ☐ Baseball
- ☐ Boat
- ☐ Brushes (2)
- ☐ Coffeepot
- ☐ Crayons (2)
- ☐ Dogs (2)
- ☐ Ducks (2)
- ☐ Fire truck
- ☐ Football
- ☐ Hammers (2)
- ☐ Helicopter
- ☐ Kite
- ☐ Knife
- ☐ Mouse
- ☐ Paddle
- ☐ Piggy bank
- ☐ Pinocchio
- ☐ Robot
- ☐ Saw
- ☐ Scissors
- ☐ Screwdriver
- ☐ Star
- ☐ Teddy bear
- ☐ Telescope
- ☐ Toy soldier
- ☐ Train engines (4)
- ☐ Triangle
- ☐ Ventriloquist
- ☐ Yo-yo

Santa decided to do his Christmas shopping in town this year. He may never try this again!

SEARCH FOR SANTA IN TOWN AND...

- ☐ Bat
- ☐ Bird
- ☐ Candle
- ☐ Cats (2)
- ☐ Dog
- ☐ Drum
- ☐ Fishing pole
- ☐ Football
- ☐ Ice-cream cone
- ☐ Indian
- ☐ Paper airplane
- ☐ Pig
- ☐ Pizza
- ☐ Rabbit
- ☐ Radio
- ☐ Roller skates
- ☐ Scrooge
- ☐ Shark
- ☐ Ship
- ☐ Shovel
- ☐ Sled
- ☐ Snowmen (3)
- ☐ Star
- ☐ Stocking
- ☐ Sword
- ☐ Target
- ☐ Tepee
- ☐ Toast
- ☐ Train engine
- ☐ Turtle
- ☐ Wreaths (8)

Elves love to play baseball. Their rules are a little different, but they have just as much fun.

SEARCH FOR SANTA AT THE BASEBALL GAME AND...

☐ Apple
☐ Baseball
☐ Baseball caps (2)
☐ Bear
☐ Bowling ball
☐ Boxing gloves
☐ Cactus
☐ Candle
☐ Clown
☐ Elephant
☐ Fish (5)
☐ Fishing pole
☐ Flowers (2)
☐ Football
☐ Ice skates
☐ Igloo
☐ Lamp
☐ Mittens
☐ Mouse
☐ Octopus
☐ Pear
☐ Rabbit
☐ Rocking chair
☐ Seal
☐ Sled
☐ Stars (3)
☐ Sunglasses
☐ Target
☐ Top hats (2)
☐ TV set
☐ Umbrella
☐ Umpires (3)
☐ Wreath

It's the morning of December 24th, and the elves are packing the sleigh. Can it take off with all that weight?

SEARCH FOR SANTA AT THE SLEIGH LOADING AND...

- ☐ Balloon
- ☐ Birdhouse
- ☐ Blimp
- ☐ Boat
- ☐ Camera
- ☐ Car
- ☐ Crayons (3)
- ☐ Flashlight
- ☐ Giraffe
- ☐ Guitar
- ☐ Hammer
- ☐ Hockey stick
- ☐ Horseshoe
- ☐ Kite
- ☐ License plate
- ☐ Mask
- ☐ Mechanic
- ☐ Needle
- ☐ Paintbrush
- ☐ Pencils (2)
- ☐ Pizza
- ☐ Rocking chair
- ☐ Sailboat
- ☐ Seal
- ☐ Skates
- ☐ Stockings (2)
- ☐ Tent
- ☐ Thread
- ☐ Train engine
- ☐ Tricycle
- ☐ Trucks (3)
- ☐ Windmill

Christmas Eve. Time to deliver the presents. Wait—something is very wrong! The sleigh has taken off and Santa's not on it!

SEARCH FOR SANTA ON CHRISTMAS EVE AND...

- ☐ Balloons (2)
- ☐ Barrel
- ☐ Bird
- ☐ Blocks
- ☐ Candy canes (3)
- ☐ Chimneys (13)
- ☐ Dog
- ☐ Drum
- ☐ Eskimo
- ☐ Happy stars (2)
- ☐ Igloo
- ☐ Ladder
- ☐ Mrs. Claus
- ☐ Robot
- ☐ Sherlock Elf
- ☐ Snow woman
- ☐ Snowman
- ☐ Teddy bear
- ☐ Telephones (2)
- ☐ Telescopes (3)
- ☐ Tent
- ☐ Truck
- ☐ TV antennas (2)
- ☐ TV set
- ☐ Yo-yo

Down the chimney he goes. But someone forgot to tell the family pet that Santa was coming!

SEARCH FOR SANTA AT HOUSE NUMBER 26 AND...

- ☐ Balloons (15)
- ☐ Bats (2)
- ☐ Bird
- ☐ Broom
- ☐ Burned out lights (6)
- ☐ Cactus
- ☐ Candles (2)
- ☐ Candy canes (2)
- ☐ Cat with a horn
- ☐ Cat in a hat
- ☐ Chairs (2)
- ☐ Christmas ornaments (4)
- ☐ Ducks (2)
- ☐ Elephant
- ☐ Fish
- ☐ Football
- ☐ Footprints
- ☐ Ghost
- ☐ Heart
- ☐ Jack-o'-lantern
- ☐ Kite
- ☐ Mitten
- ☐ Pencils (3)
- ☐ Mouse
- ☐ Pie
- ☐ Scarves (2)
- ☐ Stockings (3)
- ☐ Star
- ☐ Thermometer
- ☐ Traffic ticket
- ☐ Train engine
- ☐ Trash can
- ☐ Truck
- ☐ Trunks (2)
- ☐ Turtle
- ☐ Wreaths (4)

That night Santa visits homes all over the world, bringing Christmas cheer to all!

SEARCH FOR SANTA DELIVERING PRESENTS AND...

- ☐ Airplane
- ☐ Arrows (3)
- ☐ Bat
- ☐ Book
- ☐ Burned out lights (6)
- ☐ Candles (2)
- ☐ Doll
- ☐ Drum
- ☐ Fake Santas (7)
- ☐ Football helmet
- ☐ Ghosts (2)
- ☐ Heart
- ☐ Ice-cream cone
- ☐ Kite
- ☐ Necktie
- ☐ Roller skate
- ☐ Scarf
- ☐ Sleigh
- ☐ Spotlight
- ☐ Stars (3)
- ☐ Teddy bear
- ☐ Thermometer
- ☐ Top hat
- ☐ Train engine
- ☐ TV antenna
- ☐ Wooden soldier
- ☐ Wreaths (10)

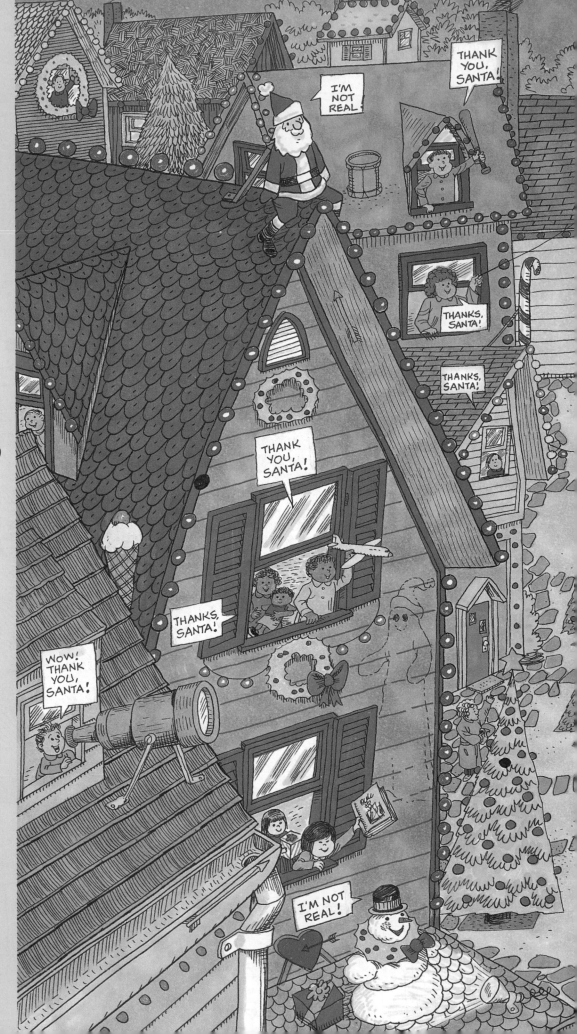

Santa is homeward bound...or is he? Can he find his way back to the North Pole?

SEARCH FOR SANTA ON EARTH AND IN SPACE AND...

- ☐ Ballons (2)
- ☐ Banana peel
- ☐ Beam
- ☐ Cactus
- ☐ Camera
- ☐ Elephant head
- ☐ Eyeglasses
- ☐ Fish (3)
- ☐ Hamburger
- ☐ Hot dog
- ☐ Igloo
- ☐ Jet sleigh
- ☐ Kite
- ☐ Magnifying glass
- ☐ Movie star
- ☐ Paper airplane
- ☐ Periscope
- ☐ Pie
- ☐ Pizza
- ☐ Rabbit
- ☐ Sherlock Holmes
- ☐ Snowmen (2)
- ☐ Super hero
- ☐ Tall elves (2)
- ☐ Telescope
- ☐ Train engine
- ☐ Unicorn

Home at last. Santa sure has a neat way of getting on and off his sleigh.

SEARCH FOR SANTA BACK AT THE NORTH POLE AND...

- ☐ Anteater
- ☐ Bats (2)
- ☐ Buffalo
- ☐ Camel
- ☐ Cheese
- ☐ Cow
- ☐ Dog
- ☐ Frog
- ☐ Flamingo
- ☐ Fox
- ☐ Kangaroo
- ☐ Kite (2)
- ☐ Ladder
- ☐ Mouse
- ☐ Owl
- ☐ Piggy bank
- ☐ Porpoise
- ☐ Rhinoceros
- ☐ Scarf
- ☐ Seal
- ☐ Star
- ☐ Toy soldier
- ☐ Umbrella
- ☐ Walruses (2)
- ☐ Wreath

The elves have asked Santa to attend a meeting. He doesn't know why, but he soon gets quite a surprise!

SEARCH FOR SANTA AT THE SURPRISE PARTY AND...

- ☐ Balloon
- ☐ Bearded elf
- ☐ Clothesline
- ☐ Clown
- ☐ Cookies
- ☐ Elephant
- ☐ Envelope
- ☐ Fish
- ☐ Giraffe
- ☐ Hammer
- ☐ Heart
- ☐ Ice-cream cone
- ☐ Kiddie pool
- ☐ Mrs. Claus
- ☐ Reindeer
- ☐ Robot
- ☐ Saw
- ☐ Scooter
- ☐ Sir Prize
- ☐ Star
- ☐ Stocking
- ☐ TV camera
- ☐ Toy duck
- ☐ Wagon

It's time for Santa and the elves to start making lots of nice gifts for next Christmas.

SEARCH FOR SANTA AT THE WORKSHOP AND...

- ☐ Apple
- ☐ Bow
- ☐ Brush
- ☐ Car
- ☐ Drumstick
- ☐ Elves in trouble (3)
- ☐ Heart
- ☐ Iron
- ☐ Owl
- ☐ Pencil
- ☐ Scissors
- ☐ Screwdriver
- ☐ Triangle
- ☐ Truck

SEARCH FOR SANTA

Here are the different Christmas pictures to look for on each of the 12 days.

Drummer Drumming

Partridge in a Pear Tree

Turtle Doves

Piper Piping

French Hen

Lord-a-Leaping

Calling Bird

Lady Dancing

Golden ring

Maid-a-Milking

Swan-a-Swimming

Goose-a-Laying

12 Days of Christmas

On the first day of Christmas my true love gave to me, a **partridge in a pear tree.** Find it hidden amongst the carolers and . . .

- ☐ Apple
- ☐ Candle
- ☐ Candy cane
- ☐ Crayon
- ☐ Dog
- ☐ Drum
- ☐ Fish
- ☐ Football
- ☐ Goose
- ☐ Heart
- ☐ Igloo
- ☐ Jack-in-the-box
- ☐ Mouse
- ☐ Paintbrush
- ☐ Paper airplane
- ☐ Piggy bank
- ☐ Rabbit
- ☐ Sailboat
- ☐ Scissors
- ☐ Sled
- ☐ Snowman
- ☐ Snow shovel
- ☐ Snow woman
- ☐ Sock
- ☐ Stars (3)
- ☐ Telescope
- ☐ Zebra

On the second day of Christmas my true love gave to me, **two turtle doves** and **a partridge in a pear tree.** Find them on this winter's day along with . . .

- ☐ Apple
- ☐ Automobile
- ☐ Bear
- ☐ Book
- ☐ Bugle
- ☐ Carrot
- ☐ Cow
- ☐ Dinosaur
- ☐ Envelope
- ☐ Fire hydrant
- ☐ Fish
- ☐ Flower
- ☐ Football
- ☐ Heart
- ☐ Helmet
- ☐ Hot dog
- ☐ Lips
- ☐ Locomotive
- ☐ Mailbox
- ☐ Mouse
- ☐ Pencil
- ☐ Pie
- ☐ Roller skate
- ☐ Saw
- ☐ Snake
- ☐ Sock
- ☐ Soda can
- ☐ Star
- ☐ Toothbrush
- ☐ Top hat
- ☐ Umbrella

On the third day of Christmas my true love gave to me, **three french hens, two turtle doves,** and **a partridge in a pear tree.** Find them in one of Santa's workshops and . . .

- ☐ Apple
- ☐ Arrow
- ☐ Baseball
- ☐ Baseball bat
- ☐ Broom
- ☐ Cactus
- ☐ Candle
- ☐ Candy cane
- ☐ Crayon
- ☐ Dog
- ☐ Duck
- ☐ Feather
- ☐ Fish
- ☐ Fork
- ☐ Hammer
- ☐ Heart
- ☐ Ice-cream cone
- ☐ Kite
- ☐ Lion
- ☐ Mermaid
- ☐ Microscope
- ☐ Mouse
- ☐ Paddle
- ☐ Pencil
- ☐ Piggy bank
- ☐ Ship
- ☐ Sled
- ☐ Star
- ☐ Wreath

On the fourth day of Christmas my true love gave to me, **four calling birds, three french hens, two turtle doves, and a partridge in a pear tree.** Find them at this school presentation of *A Christmas Carol* as well as . . . .

- ☐ Apple
- ☐ Baseball
- ☐ Book
- ☐ Broom
- ☐ Candle
- ☐ Christmas tree
- ☐ Crown
- ☐ Drum
- ☐ Elf
- ☐ Envelope
- ☐ Fish
- ☐ Flower
- ☐ Flying bat
- ☐ Goose
- ☐ Heart

- ☐ Key
- ☐ Ladder
- ☐ Lost sock
- ☐ Lost tie
- ☐ Owl
- ☐ Pencil
- ☐ Pie
- ☐ Pumpkin
- ☐ Seal
- ☐ Sled
- ☐ Snowman
- ☐ Squirrel
- ☐ Wagon
- ☐ Wreath

On the fifth day of Christmas my true love gave to me, **five golden rings, four calling birds, three french hens, two turtle doves,** and **a partridge in a pear tree.** Find them at the elves' snowball game and . . .

- ☐ Automobile
- ☐ Balloons (2)
- ☐ Barrel
- ☐ Dogs (2)
- ☐ Fish (3)
- ☐ Giraffe
- ☐ Hockey stick
- ☐ Horseshoe
- ☐ Igloo
- ☐ Kites (2)
- ☐ Paintbrush
- ☐ Rocking chair
- ☐ Sailboat
- ☐ Stars (2)
- ☐ Teddy bear
- ☐ Telephone receiver
- ☐ Telescope
- ☐ Tents (3)
- ☐ Truck
- ☐ Turtle
- ☐ Wreath
- ☐ Yo-yo

On the sixth day of Christmas my true love gave to me, **six geese-a-laying, five golden rings, four calling birds, three french hens, two turtle doves,** and a **partridge in a pear tree.** Find them at this tree decorating party. Also find . . .

- ☐ Apple
- ☐ Baseball bat
- ☐ Candle
- ☐ Drum
- ☐ Envelope
- ☐ Fish
- ☐ Flower
- ☐ Flying bat
- ☐ Football
- ☐ Ghost
- ☐ Happy monster
- ☐ Heart
- ☐ Kangaroo
- ☐ Key
- ☐ Moon face
- ☐ Paintbrush
- ☐ Rabbit
- ☐ Toothbrush
- ☐ Turtle
- ☐ TV set

BAKERY   FLOWERS   TOYS

On the seventh day of Christmas my true love gave to me, **seven swans-a-swimming, six geese-a-laying, five golden rings, four calling birds, three french hens, two turtle doves,** and **a partridge in a pear tree.** Find them all at this tropical Christmas and . . .

- [ ] Automobile
- [ ] Cactus
- [ ] Candle
- [ ] Candy cane
- [ ] Elephant
- [ ] Envelope
- [ ] Hammer
- [ ] Horn
- [ ] Hot dog
- [ ] Key
- [ ] Mouse
- [ ] Oar
- [ ] Package
- [ ] Party hat
- [ ] Pencil
- [ ] Sailboat
- [ ] Saw
- [ ] Seal
- [ ] Shark fin
- [ ] Shovel
- [ ] Star
- [ ] Telescope
- [ ] Tent
- [ ] Tick-tack-toe
- [ ] Wreath

On the eighth day of Christmas my true love gave to me, **eight maids-a-milking, seven swans-a-swimming, six geese-a-laying, five golden rings, four calling birds, three french hens, two turtle doves,** and **a partridge in a pear tree.** Find them in this busy shopping mall plus . . .

☐ Airplane
☐ Automobile
☐ Balloon
☐ Book
☐ Cactus
☐ Drum

☐ Elephants (2)
☐ Fish
☐ Ghost
☐ Heart
☐ Horn
☐ Lost socks (3)

☐ Mitten
☐ Mouse
☐ Necktie
☐ Pencil
☐ Rabbit
☐ Unicorn

On the ninth day of Christmas my true love gave to me, **nine ladies dancing, eight maids-a-milking, seven swans-a-swimming, six geese-a-laying, five golden rings, four calling birds, three french hens, two turtle doves,** and **a partridge in a pear tree.** Find them in this snowstorm as well as . . .

- ☐ Cactus
- ☐ Camel
- ☐ Camera
- ☐ Candle
- ☐ Candy cane
- ☐ Cheese
- ☐ Clothespin
- ☐ Clown
- ☐ Coffeepot
- ☐ Cow
- ☐ Crayon
- ☐ Heart
- ☐ Igloo
- ☐ Kite
- ☐ Lips
- ☐ Rabbit
- ☐ Sled
- ☐ Star

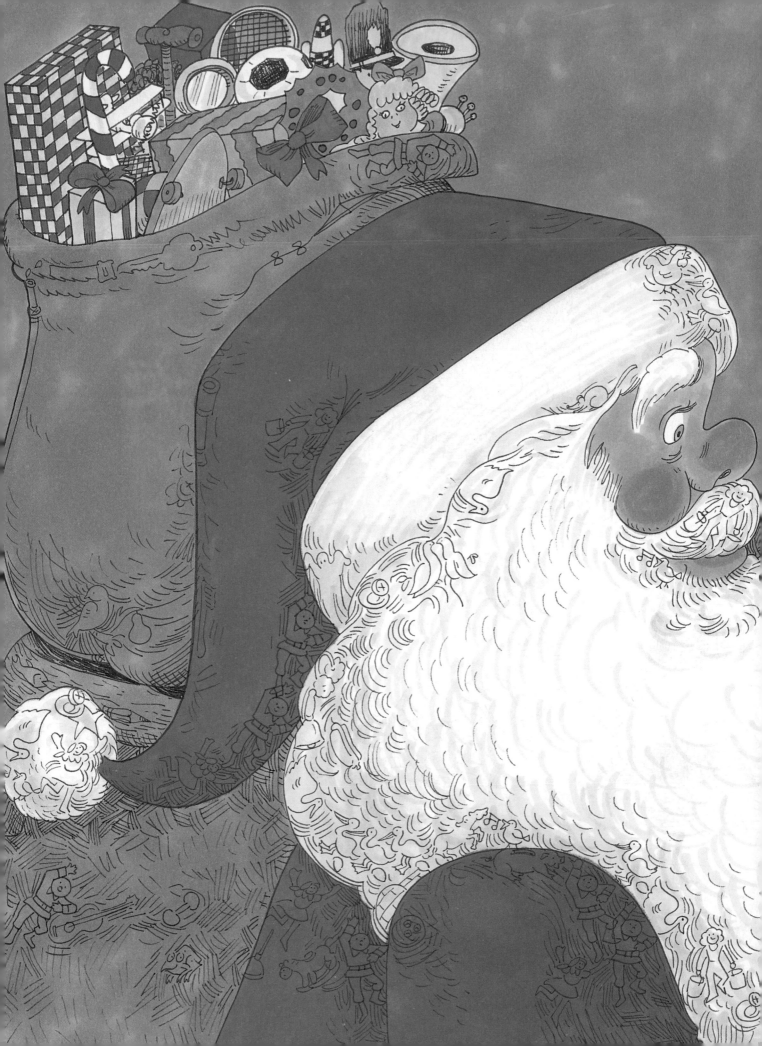

On the tenth day of Christmas my true love gave to me, **ten lords-a-leaping, nine ladies dancing, eight maids-a-milking, seven swans-a-swimming, six geese-a-laying, five golden rings, four calling birds, three french hens, two turtle doves,** and **a partridge in a pear tree.** Find them hidden in this picture of Santa checking his list. Also find . . .

- ☐ Balloon
- ☐ Barbell
- ☐ Bell
- ☐ Bowling ball
- ☐ Christmas tree
- ☐ Earmuffs
- ☐ Fish
- ☐ Flower
- ☐ Football
- ☐ Frog
- ☐ Garden hose
- ☐ Ghost
- ☐ Guitar
- ☐ Horse

- ☐ Hot dog
- ☐ Igloo
- ☐ Key
- ☐ Lion
- ☐ Oilcan
- ☐ Pencil
- ☐ Piggy bank
- ☐ Rabbit
- ☐ Rocking horse
- ☐ Sailboat
- ☐ Saw
- ☐ Teddy bear
- ☐ Telescope
- ☐ Toothbrush

On the eleventh day of Christmas my true love gave to me, **eleven pipers piping, ten lords-a-leaping, nine ladies dancing, eight maids-a-milking, seven swans-a-swimming, six geese-a-laying, five golden rings, four calling birds, three french hens, two turtle doves,** and **a partridge in a pear tree.** Find them as Santa starts his Christmas Eve journey along with . . .

- ☐ Apple
- ☐ Arrow
- ☐ Banana
- ☐ Boot
- ☐ Carrot
- ☐ Dog
- ☐ Eyeglasses
- ☐ Football
- ☐ Football helmet
- ☐ Golf club
- ☐ Helicopter
- ☐ Hockey stick
- ☐ Jack-o'-lantern
- ☐ Lamp
- ☐ Laundry
- ☐ Light bulb
- ☐ Scissors
- ☐ Seal
- ☐ Straw hat
- ☐ Tent
- ☐ Toaster
- ☐ Top hat
- ☐ Turtle
- ☐ Umbrella
- ☐ Watering can

ASIA

EUROPE

NORTH AND SOUTH AMERICA

AFRICA

On the twelfth day of Christmas my true love gave to me:

- ☐ 12 Drummers Drumming
- ☐ 11 Pipers Piping
- ☐ 10 Lords-a-Leaping
- ☐ 9 Ladies Dancing
- ☐ 8 Maids-a-Milking
- ☐ 7 Swans-a-Swimming
- ☐ 6 Geese-a-Laying

□ 5 Golden Rings
□ 4 Calling Birds
□ 3 French Hens
□ 2 Turtle Doves
□ and a Partridge in a Pear Tree!

Can you find them all?

Search for Santa's Helpers

Fee   Fi

Fo   Fun

The elves made so many gifts this year that they're running out of places in which to store them.

SEARCH FOR FEE, FI, FO, AND FUN AT THE GIFT STORAGE CENTER AND...

- ☐ Baseball bat
- ☐ Bell
- ☐ Book
- ☐ Bowling ball
- ☐ Candy canes (3)
- ☐ Clown
- ☐ Duck
- ☐ Earmuffs (2 pairs)
- ☐ Elves with beards (3)
- ☐ Empty warehouse
- ☐ Fishing pole
- ☐ Flower
- ☐ Footballs (2)
- ☐ Horse
- ☐ Igloo
- ☐ Jack-in-the-box
- ☐ Kite
- ☐ Lion
- ☐ Mouse
- ☐ Rabbits (2)
- ☐ Robot
- ☐ Santa Claus
- ☐ Scarecrow
- ☐ Scarves (8)
- ☐ Shoemaker
- ☐ Skier
- ☐ Snake
- ☐ Telescopes (2)
- ☐ Thermometer
- ☐ Toy elephants (3)
- ☐ Train engine
- ☐ Turtle
- ☐ Unicorn
- ☐ Watch

Fee Fi Fo Fun

This is the place where all those fancy bows and ribbons are made.

SEARCH FOR FEE, FI, FO, AND FUN AT THE BIG BOW WORKS AND...

- ☐ Airplane
- ☐ Balloon
- ☐ Bell
- ☐ Bunny
- ☐ Cat
- ☐ Clown
- ☐ Cow
- ☐ Crayon
- ☐ Cup
- ☐ Dog
- ☐ Elephant
- ☐ Flying bat
- ☐ Garden hose
- ☐ Ghost
- ☐ Globe
- ☐ Guitar
- ☐ Hot dog
- ☐ Jack-o'-lantern
- ☐ Jack-in-the-box
- ☐ Jump rope
- ☐ Lollipops (3)
- ☐ Oil can
- ☐ Package
- ☐ Paint bucket
- ☐ Panda
- ☐ Pencil
- ☐ Piggy bank
- ☐ Robot
- ☐ Sailboat
- ☐ Snake
- ☐ Sunglasses
- ☐ Super-hero doll
- ☐ Tape measure
- ☐ Truck
- ☐ Unicorn
- ☐ Wreath
- ☐ Yellow star

Fee | Fi
Fo | Fun

The elves are hard at work making lots of wonderful gifts for Santa to deliver on Christmas Eve.

SEARCH FOR FEE, FI, FO, AND FUN AT SANTA'S WORKSHOP AND...

☐ Alien spaceship
☐ Airplanes (2)
☐ Astronaut
☐ Banana peel
☐ Barbell
☐ Bird
☐ Bottle
☐ Bowling ball
☐ Broom
☐ Candle
☐ Chimneys (3)
☐ Clock
☐ Fish
☐ Flower
☐ Frog
☐ Green feather
☐ Hockey stick
☐ Ice skate
☐ Juggler
☐ Magnifying glass
☐ Mallets (2)
☐ Moose head
☐ Mouse
☐ Nets (3)
☐ Race car
☐ Rocket ship
☐ Rocking chair
☐ Saddle
☐ Sailor hat
☐ Saw
☐ Screw
☐ Skateboard
☐ Sock
☐ Surfboard
☐ Tent
☐ Toy soldier
☐ TV antenna

The card makers are really busy this time of year.

SEARCH FOR FEE, FI, FO, AND FUN AT THE CHRISTMAS CARD FACTORY AND...

☐ Arrow
☐ Balloon
☐ Beachball
☐ Bird
☐ Birdhouse
☐ Bone
☐ Broom
☐ Candle
☐ Cat
☐ Chair
☐ Cloud
☐ Curtains
☐ Dog
☐ Elephant
☐ Fake snow
☐ Feather
☐ Fish
☐ Flower
☐ Hammer
☐ Heart
☐ Ice skates
☐ Igloo
☐ Kite
☐ Lights (2)
☐ Models (4)
☐ Number 26
☐ Paint bucket
☐ Paintbrush
☐ Pencil
☐ Pizza
☐ Scarf
☐ Scissors
☐ Shovels (2)
☐ Star
☐ Turtle
☐ Wagon
☐ Wreath

Fee Fi Fo Fun

Everybody loves to sing Christmas songs, especially the elves.

SEARCH FOR FEE, FI, FO, AND FUN AT THE CHRISTMAS CAROL SING-ALONG AND...

☐ Angel
☐ Balloons (5)
☐ Baseball
☐ Baseball cap
☐ Bells (2)
☐ Cactus
☐ Candy canes (2)
☐ Carrot
☐ Clothespin
☐ Deer
☐ Duck
☐ "Elfis"
☐ Elves wearing glasses (4)
☐ Elves with beards (2)
☐ Feather
☐ Flute
☐ Flying carpet
☐ Football helmet
☐ Horse
☐ Ice skates
☐ Jack-in-the-box
☐ Kettle drum
☐ Parrot
☐ Penguin
☐ Pillow
☐ Pizza
☐ Rabbits (2)
☐ School bag
☐ Singing tree
☐ Skier
☐ Torn gloves
☐ Tuba
☐ Watering can
☐ Wreaths (3)

Fee Fi Fo Fun

With a little teamwork, and a lot of elves, making wreaths is easy and fun to do.

SEARCH FOR FEE, FI, FO, AND FUN AT THE WREATH MAKERS AND...

- ☐ Balloon
- ☐ Bird
- ☐ Candle
- ☐ Candy cane
- ☐ Chair
- ☐ Christmas stockings (2)
- ☐ Crayon
- ☐ Crown
- ☐ Deer
- ☐ Doors
- ☐ Duck
- ☐ Falling star
- ☐ Fish
- ☐ Football
- ☐ Garden hose
- ☐ Ice skates
- ☐ Jack-in-the-box
- ☐ Jars of glue (3)
- ☐ Ladder
- ☐ Light bulbs (3)
- ☐ Mouse
- ☐ Oil can
- ☐ Paintbrush
- ☐ Pencils (2)
- ☐ Picture frame
- ☐ Pizza
- ☐ Propeller
- ☐ Rake
- ☐ Rejected wreaths
- ☐ Roller skates
- ☐ Shovel
- ☐ Snake
- ☐ Top hat
- ☐ Turtle
- ☐ TV set
- ☐ Umbrella
- ☐ Wagon
- ☐ Watering can

Fee	Fi
Fo	Fun

So many gifts...so little time... and they all have to be wrapped before Christmas Eve!

SEARCH FOR FEE, FI, FO, AND FUN AT THE GIFT WRAPPING DEPARTMENT AND...

- ☐ Airplane
- ☐ Arrows (2)
- ☐ Banana peel
- ☐ Baseball
- ☐ Basketball
- ☐ Books (3)
- ☐ Boots
- ☐ Candy canes (3)
- ☐ Carrot
- ☐ Christmas stockings (3)
- ☐ Computer
- ☐ Doll
- ☐ Drum
- ☐ Flower
- ☐ Footballs (2)
- ☐ Golf club
- ☐ Horn
- ☐ Kites (3)
- ☐ Lamp
- ☐ Lunch box
- ☐ Pencils (2)
- ☐ Piggy bank
- ☐ Rabbit
- ☐ Rocking horse
- ☐ Sailboat
- ☐ Scissors
- ☐ Snowmen (2)
- ☐ Star
- ☐ Tennis racket
- ☐ Tent
- ☐ Trampoline
- ☐ Tricycle
- ☐ Wrapped elf
- ☐ Wrapped gift

Fee Fi Fo Fun

'Tis the week before Christmas and, at the North Pole, not a creature is working, not even a mole. Why not? Because it's time for the elves' Christmas party!

SEARCH FOR FEE, FI, FO, AND FUN AT THE CHRISTMAS PARTY AND...

☐ Balloon
☐ Banana
☐ Bell
☐ Birds (2)
☐ Bows (4)
☐ Broom
☐ Clock
☐ Chef's hat
☐ Deer
☐ Dog
☐ Dracula
☐ Eyeglasses
    (2 pairs)
☐ Feather
☐ Fish
☐ Flowerpot
☐ Football helmet
☐ Guitar
☐ Igloo
☐ Jack-o'-lantern
☐ Loudspeaker
☐ Mama Claus
☐ Mouse
☐ Piano
☐ Pitcher
☐ Rocking chair
☐ Roller skates (2)
☐ Scrooge
☐ Seal
☐ Straw
☐ Top hats (2)
☐ Train engine
☐ Turtles (2)
☐ Umbrella

Fee Fi Fo Fun

What a wonderful place to work. It looks like a delicious crop this year!

SEARCH FOR FEE, FI, FO, AND FUN AT THE CANDY CANE FARM AND...

☐ Airplane
☐ Ax
☐ Barn
☐ Barrel
☐ Baseball bat
☐ Birds (7)
☐ Broom
☐ Carrot
☐ Condo
☐ Crayon
☐ Crown
☐ Dog
☐ Elephant
☐ Evergreen tree
☐ Goat
☐ Goose
☐ Hammock
☐ Helicopter
☐ Hot dog
☐ Kangaroo
☐ Laundry
☐ Mailbox
☐ Mouse
☐ Pail
☐ Paint bucket
☐ Pencil
☐ Pig
☐ Polka-dotted cane
☐ Rabbit
☐ Reject basket
☐ Shovel
☐ Sled
☐ Snowball fight
☐ Straw hat
☐ Stripeless cane
☐ Tractor
☐ Wagon
☐ Watering can
☐ Windmill

Fee	Fi
Fo	Fun

The big night—Christmas Eve—is finally here! Everyone is helping to pack the sleigh, and Santa is ready to go!

SEARCH FOR FEE, FI, FO, AND FUN ON CHRISTMAS EVE AND...

- ☐ Apple
- ☐ Arrow
- ☐ Baseball
- ☐ Basket
- ☐ Bell
- ☐ Boots (2 pairs)
- ☐ Camera
- ☐ Candelabra
- ☐ Crayons (3)
- ☐ Drum
- ☐ Earmuffs
- ☐ Envelope
- ☐ Hockey stick
- ☐ Hoe
- ☐ Igloo
- ☐ Knitting needles
- ☐ Lollipop
- ☐ Picture frame
- ☐ Polka-dotted bow
- ☐ Propellers (2)
- ☐ Robot
- ☐ Sailboat
- ☐ Shovel
- ☐ Slide
- ☐ Stars (3)
- ☐ Stowaway
- ☐ Toaster
- ☐ Train engines (2)
- ☐ Umbrella
- ☐ Weather vane
- ☐ Wheelbarrow
- ☐ Wreath

Christmas greetings to you from Fee, Fi, Fo, Fun, and their friends:

Freddie   Hector
Lisa   Laura
Susie   Santa
Frankie   Donald
Bunny Honey   Sam

SEARCH FOR SANTA'S HELPERS

Santa Claus has his sleigh loaded with gifts for his long Christmas Eve journey. He's also hidden lots of things for you to find below.

☐ Automobile
☐ Bell
☐ Bird
☐ Book
☐ Clown face
☐ Dog
☐ Duck
☐ Envelope

☐ Fish
☐ Fork
☐ Ghost
☐ Hammer
☐ Hearts (2)
☐ Igloo
☐ Jack-o'-lantern

☐ Key
☐ Kite
☐ Lips
☐ Paintbrush
☐ Pencil
☐ Pick
☐ Sailboat

☐ Snow shovel
☐ Spoon
☐ Star
☐ Tepee
☐ Tree ornament
☐ Turtle
☐ Umbrella

Up, up, and away goes Santa as he soars through the sky delivering gifts around the world. Children of all ages await his arrival, but can you find the following hidden pictures before he makes his first stop?

- [ ] Arrow
- [ ] Baseball
- [ ] Bat
- [ ] Coffeepot
- [ ] Crayon
- [ ] Dog
- [ ] Duck
- [ ] Football
- [ ] Ghost
- [ ] Hammer
- [ ] Heart
- [ ] Helicopter
- [ ] Hot-air balloon
- [ ] Ice-cream cone
- [ ] Igloo

- [ ] Knife
- [ ] Locomotive
- [ ] Mouse
- [ ] Paintbrush
- [ ] Pig
- [ ] Pillow
- [ ] Pinocchio
- [ ] Ring
- [ ] Saw
- [ ] Scissors
- [ ] Screwdriver
- [ ] Ship
- [ ] Surfboard
- [ ] Telescope
- [ ] Wreath

HE MAKES THE WHOLE WORLD HAPPY!

Down the chimney Santa goes with his bag of gifts.
Quickly, before he lands, find . . .

- ☐ Bat
- ☐ Bird
- ☐ Book
- ☐ Cactus
- ☐ Chair
- ☐ Crayon
- ☐ Dog
- ☐ Duck
- ☐ Elephant head
- ☐ Fish
- ☐ Ghost
- ☐ Heart
- ☐ Igloo
- ☐ Jack-o´-lantern
- ☐ Kangaroo
- ☐ Key
- ☐ Kite
- ☐ Lamp
- ☐ Mouse
- ☐ Owl
- ☐ Pencil
- ☐ Pie
- ☐ Ring
- ☐ Roller skate
- ☐ Sailboat
- ☐ Saw
- ☐ Stocking
- ☐ Telescope
- ☐ Turtle
- ☐ Unicorn

THERE IS SANTA!

WE'LL SURPRISE HIM WHEN HE COMES HERE!

Children have always tried to surprise Santa when he arrives. You can surprise him by finding the hidden objects below.

☐ Baseball
☐ Baseball cap
☐ Birds (2)
☐ Bowling ball
☐ Broom
☐ Cactus
☐ Candle
☐ Carrot
☐ Elves (2)
☐ Fish
☐ Flower
☐ Ghost
☐ Ice skate
☐ Ice-cream cone
☐ Light bulb

☐ Mailbox
☐ Mitten
☐ Octopus
☐ Paintbrush
☐ Pumpkin
☐ Rabbit
☐ Rocking chair
☐ Sailboat
☐ Seal
☐ Sled
☐ Star
☐ Toothbrush
☐ Top hat
☐ Turtle
☐ Umbrella

HE'LL BE HERE SOON.

Oh, no! They fell asleep. Somehow, Santa always knows to come when kids can't stay awake any longer. But if you're still awake, find . . .

- ☐ Bird
- ☐ Book
- ☐ Candy canes (2)
- ☐ Dog
- ☐ Doll
- ☐ Drum
- ☐ Elf
- ☐ Flashlight
- ☐ Football
- ☐ Football helmet
- ☐ Guitar
- ☐ Hammer
- ☐ Heart
- ☐ Hockey stick

- ☐ Horn
- ☐ Mermaid
- ☐ Mouse
- ☐ Owl
- ☐ Pencil
- ☐ Pie
- ☐ Quarter moon
- ☐ Rocking horse
- ☐ Roller skate
- ☐ Teddy bear
- ☐ Tent
- ☐ Truck
- ☐ Trunk
- ☐ Turtle
- ☐ Wooden soldier

Santa is flying over a tropical island when ... oops! Who could that present be for? Maybe it's for you, but first you must find the hidden pictures below.

- [ ] Balloon
- [ ] Barrel
- [ ] Baseball bat
- [ ] Broom
- [ ] Cactus
- [ ] Candle
- [ ] Chair
- [ ] Dog
- [ ] Drum
- [ ] Duck

- [ ] Fish (2)
- [ ] Flying bat
- [ ] Ghost
- [ ] Heart
- [ ] Key
- [ ] Ladder
- [ ] Mitten
- [ ] Paintbrush
- [ ] Pencil
- [ ] Pie

- [ ] Ring
- [ ] Sailboat
- [ ] Saw
- [ ] Stocking
- [ ] Telephone
- [ ] Tent
- [ ] Truck
- [ ] Umbrella
- [ ] Wreath

YOU DROPPED SOMETHING, SANTA.

Santa has landed his sleigh to look for the lost teddy bear. Help him find it and . . .

☐ Arrow
☐ Automobile
☐ Banana
☐ Baseball cap
☐ Candy cane
☐ Chair
☐ Cup
☐ Fire hydrant

☐ Fish
☐ Ghost
☐ Hammer
☐ Hot dog
☐ Ice-cream cone
☐ Igloo
☐ Jack-o´-lantern
☐ Kite

☐ Mouse
☐ Music note
☐ Paintbrush
☐ Pencil
☐ Ring
☐ Robot
☐ Shovel
☐ Snake

☐ Star
☐ Teddy bear
☐ Telescope
☐ Toothbrush
☐ Trash can
☐ Trunk
☐ Turtle
☐ TV set

Santa Claus has finished delivering his presents just in time, as the sun rises on Christmas morning. Before you see what Santa's brought, find . . .

- ☐ Airplane
- ☐ Apple
- ☐ Axe
- ☐ Basketball
- ☐ Bell
- ☐ Boot
- ☐ Camera
- ☐ Candelabra
- ☐ Carrot
- ☐ Clown
- ☐ Crayon

- ☐ Earmuffs
- ☐ Elephant
- ☐ Envelope
- ☐ Hoe
- ☐ Horn
- ☐ Iron
- ☐ Kangaroo
- ☐ Mailbox
- ☐ Pail
- ☐ Paint bucket

- ☐ Picture frame
- ☐ Pig
- ☐ Pitcher
- ☐ Rabbit
- ☐ Stars (4)
- ☐ Sunglasses
- ☐ Toaster
- ☐ Top hat
- ☐ Wagon
- ☐ Wheelbarrow

Santa is back at his home, but everyone and everything seem to be hidden.
Can you find the following ?

☐ Airplane
☐ Automobiles (2)
☐ Baseball bat
☐ Bottle
☐ Candle
☐ Comb
☐ Cowboy hat
☐ Crayon
☐ Cup
☐ Duck
☐ Elf
☐ Fish
☐ Flying bat
☐ Football
☐ Frog

☐ Ghost
☐ Guitar
☐ Hot dog
☐ Ice skate
☐ Key
☐ Locomotive
☐ Magnifying glass
☐ Paintbrush
☐ Pencil
☐ Piggy bank
☐ Snail
☐ Tent
☐ Tree ornament
☐ Turtle

Santa opens the door to the toy shop and ... Surprise! Children from all over the world had written Mrs. Claus to see if they could come to the North Pole and give Santa a **SUPER SURPRISE!** But wait! This book is not over until you find . . .

- ☐ Apple
- ☐ Bell
- ☐ Bird
- ☐ Book
- ☐ Bowling pin
- ☐ Candle
- ☐ Candy cane
- ☐ Drum

- ☐ Duck
- ☐ Fish
- ☐ Fork
- ☐ Kite
- ☐ Medal
- ☐ Moon face
- ☐ Mouse
- ☐ Oilcan

- ☐ Owl
- ☐ Paintbrush
- ☐ Rabbit
- ☐ Rocketship
- ☐ Roller skate
- ☐ Sailboat
- ☐ Saw
- ☐ Scarecrow

- ☐ Screwdriver
- ☐ Sock
- ☐ Stars (2)
- ☐ Toothbrush
- ☐ Tree ornament
- ☐ Truck
- ☐ Turtle
- ☐ Unicorn

WELCOME HOME SANTA!

YOU BROUGHT US GIFTS... NOW WE HAVE SOME FOR YOU!